A Look at Books

Learning to Count by Tens to 50

D. J. Cortland

Rosen Classroom Books & Materials
New York

A **library** is a place where you can go to find books.

Schools have libraries. Towns have libraries. Big cities have libraries, too.

You can find books with stories at the library. You can also find books about real people and places.

What do you like to read about? You
can find books about many things at
the library.

Do you like to read about animals? We see 10 books about animals at the library.

10 books

Do you like to read about places? We see 10 books about places. Now we can count 20 books altogether.

10 books + 10 books = 20 books

Do you like to read about **famous** people?

We see 10 books about famous people.

Now we can count 30 books altogether.

10 books + 10 books + 10 books = 30 books

Do you like to read about sports? We see 10 books about sports. Now we can count 40 books altogether.

10 books + 10 books + 10 books + 10 books = 40 books

Do you like to read stories? We see 10 books with stories. Now we can count 50 books altogether!

10 books + 10 books + 10 books + 10 books + 10 books = 50 books

You can learn a lot at the library. Do you know where the library is in your city or town?

Glossary

famous (FAY-muhs) Very well-known.

library (LIE-brer-ee) A place that will lend
   you books.